Children's Celebrations

Ian Rohr

Smart Apple Media
P.O. Box 3263
Mankato, MN, 56002

First published in 2010 by
MACMILLAN EDUCATION AUSTRALIA PTY LTD
15–19 Claremont St, South Yarra, Australia 3141

Visit our web site at www.macmillan.com.au or go directly to www.macmillanlibrary.com.au

Associated companies and representatives throughout the world.

Copyright © Ian Rohr 2010

Library of Congress Cataloging-in-Publication Data

Rohr, Ian.
    Children's celebrations / Ian Rohr.
        p. cm. -- (Celebrations around the world)
    Includes index.
    ISBN 978-1-59920-535-9 (library binding)
    1. Children's festivals--Juvenile literature. I. Title.
    GT3933.R63 2011
    394.26--dc22
                                    2009042138

Publisher: Carmel Heron
Managing Editor: Vanessa Lanaway
Editor: Michaela Forster
Proofreader: Kirstie Innes-Will
Designer: Kerri Wilson (cover and text)
Page layout: Pier Vido
Photo researcher: Wendy Duncan
Production Controller: Vanessa Johnson

Manufactured in China by Macmillan Production (Asia) Ltd.
Kwun Tong, Kowloon, Hong Kong
Supplier Code: CP January 2010

Acknowledgments

The author and the publisher are grateful to the following for permission to reproduce copyright material:

Cover photograph: Children blowing out candles on a birthday cake, © iStockphoto/Rich Legg

Classical Movements Inc. Rhapsody Children's Music Festival: Vienna, Salzburg & Prague, 14; © Heide Benser/Corbis, 4; © G. Bowater/Corbis, 13; © Philippe Giraud/Corbis, 19; © Chris Hellier/Corbis, 20; © Bob Krist/Corbis, 15; © Jupiter Unlimited/ Thinkstock Images, 5; © Image Source/Getty Images, 12; © Akira Kaede/Photodisc/Getty Images, 23; © Guang Niu/Getty Images, 8; © Issouf Sanogo/AFP/Getty Images, 24; © Zhao Jing/ChinaFotoPress/Getty Images, 6; © iStockphoto/Rich Legg, 1, 10; Courtesy Lola Kenya Screen, 25; Lonely Planet Images/Felix Hug, 11; Newspix/David Clark, 17; Newspix/Daniel Wilkins, 16; Ottawa International Children's Festival/Binary Rhyme, 28, 29; photolibrary/Britain On View, 7; photolibrary/Tim Hall, 18; photolibrary/Robin Laurance, 22; photolibrary/Alamy/Claudia Wiens, 21; © Shutterstock/Kevin Renes, 30; © UN Photo/Fardin Waez, 9; Uri Gordon, 26, 27.

While every care has been taken to trace and acknowledge copyright, the publisher tenders their apologies for any accidental infringement where copyright has proved untraceable. Where the attempt has been unsuccessful, the publisher welcomes information that would redress the situation.

Contents

When a word is printed in **bold**, you can look up its meaning in the Glossary on page 31.

Celebrations

Celebrations are events that are held on special occasions. Some are events from the past that are still celebrated. Others celebrate important times in our lives or activities, such as music.

Birthdays are special events that many people celebrate.

Some celebrations involve only a few people.
Others involve whole cities or countries.
Large celebrations take place across the world.

New Year's Eve is celebrated all around
the world with fireworks.

What Are Children's Celebrations?

Children's celebrations are events especially for children. They can be small, such as birthday parties. There are also children's festivals, which are big celebrations.

Children's festivals are celebrations for big groups of children.

Large children's celebrations often involve music, books, or movies. Organizing a big celebration involves many people and a lot of planning.

Children's festivals have activities and performances especially for children, such as clown acts.

Universal Children's Day

Universal Children's Day celebrates friendship among children from different **cultures**. It was first started by an organization called the **United Nations** in 1954. The celebration looks at children's **rights**.

Fun events, such as performances by unicyclists, are part of Universal Children's Day.

Universal Children's Day is celebrated on November 20 each year. It looks at ways to improve the health and education of children.

On Universal Children's Day, many teachers tell students about children's rights.

Birthday Celebrations

Birthdays celebrate the day a person was born. They have been celebrated for thousands of years. Many children like birthdays because they are a day just for them.

Children often celebrate their birthday with their friends.

Birthdays are celebrated in many countries. However, not all religions or cultures celebrate birthdays. Some religions celebrate **name days** instead of birthdays.

Birthdays are celebrated by children from many religions and cultures.

Birthdays are often celebrated with a party. A birthday cake and presents are part of the celebrations. Children's birthday parties often include games.

Pass the gift is a popular game at children's birthday parties.

Birthday celebrations are not just for children.
People often have a big party when they turn
21 or 50 years old.

Turning 100 is
a very special
birthday.

Music Festivals

The Rhapsody! Children's Music Festival is held in Europe each year. Children's **choirs** from around the world perform at concerts. Sometimes the choirs sing with an **orchestra**.

A highlight of the Rhapsody! Children's Music Festival is when the choirs sing together.

The Pacific Rim Children's Chorus Festival is held for young people from the Pacific region. At the festival they learn about singing, playing instruments, storytelling, and dance from the Pacific.

At the festival, children perform dances from the Pacific region.

Book Week

Book Week is a celebration that encourages children to read books. It is celebrated in many places around the world. Schools and libraries hold events such as competitions and storytelling.

Storytelling is held in libraries during Book Week.

In Australia, Book Week has a different **theme** every year. Past themes have included "celebrate with stories" and "reading rocks!" It is one of the oldest children's festivals in Australia.

Book Week activities include dressing up as characters from books.

Mid-Autumn Children's Festival, Vietnam

The Mid-Autumn Children's Festival is held in Vietnam when the fall moon is full. It is very old, and is called Tet Trung Thu (say *tet-troong-thoo*).

Colorful lanterns are part of the Mid-Autumn Children's Festival.

During the festival, children gather together, wear masks, and bang drums. They also eat **mooncakes**, listen to fairy tales, and watch dragon dances.

Children parade through the streets and sing loudly during the Mid-Autumn Children's Festival.

Children's Day, Turkey

Children's Day is held in Turkey on April 23 each year. On Children's Day, children rule the country. The day celebrates the importance of children.

On Children's Day, many children dress in the Turkish national costume.

Children's Day also involves dancing and giving presents. Many children come from other countries to stay with Turkish families. Children's Day is known as Egemenlik Bayrami (say *eh-ge-men-lik by-rah-muh*).

On Children's Day, music performers dress in red and white (the Turkish national colors).

Children's Day, Japan

Children's Day, known as Kodomo no hi, is held in Japan on May 5. It celebrates children and their mothers. Rice cakes and other sweets are eaten on Children's Day.

Ceremonies held on Children's Day celebrate children and their happiness.

Families with sons hang kites outside their homes.
The kites are shaped like carp, a strong fish.
Parents hope their sons will grow up to be strong
like carp.

Parents fly one kite for every son in the
family on Children's Day.

Lola Kenya Screen, Kenya

Lola Kenya Screen is a film festival for children. It celebrates films that are written and made by children. Lola Kenya Screen is held every year in Kenya in Africa.

Children gather to watch films at Lola Kenya Screen.

At the festival, films are made by children at **workshops**. Children also help select the films shown at the festival. They vote for the ones they think are the best.

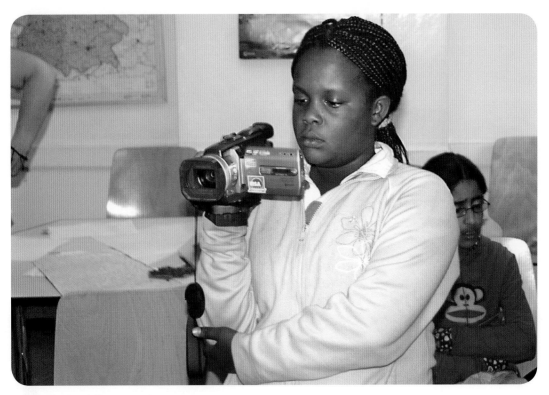

At Lola Kenya Screen, children learn how to make short films.

Children's Fair, Argentina

The Children's Fair (La Feria de los Chicos) takes place every year in Argentina. It means "the fair of the boys," but this celebration is for all children.

Thousands of visitors enjoy performances and stalls at the Children's Fair.

There are many different activities at the fair. These include theater, circus acts, and puppet shows. There are also cooking classes and a storytelling corner.

Music performances are popular events at the Children's Fair.

International Children's Festival, Canada

The International Children's Festival is held in Canada. It takes place in June each year and runs for five days. The festival has many events.

Circus acts are popular at the International Children's Festival.

Many school groups attend performances at the International Children's Festival. The children learn about music, art, and drama from other countries.

Some music performances include children from the audience.

Try This!

Find the answers to these questions in the book.
(You can check your answers on page 31.)

1 Where is the Mid-Autumn Children's Festival celebrated?

2 Who takes part in the Rhapsody! Children's Music Festival?

3 Where do children rule the country for a day?

4 What does Universal Children's Day aim to do?

5 What do some religions celebrate instead of birthdays?

Try This Activity

Next time you celebrate a special occasion with your friends or family, ask yourself:

* Why are you celebrating?
* How long have people been celebrating this event?
* Are there other places in the world where people celebrate the event?

Glossary

choirs	groups of people singing together, often without any instruments
cultures	ways of living
mooncakes	sweet cakes
name days	days when people celebrate the saint who shares their name
orchestra	a group of musicians playing instruments
rights	things people should be allowed to have or do
theme	main idea
United Nations	an organization that most countries belong to
workshops	classes where people are taught skills

Answers to the Quiz on Page 30

1 Vietnam
2 Children's choirs from around the world
3 Turkey
4 Celebrate friendship among children from different cultures, and improve the health and education of all children
5 Name days

Index